LIFE IN THE SPECIAL FORCES

LIFE IN THE
MARINE FORCE RECON

by Jenny Crooks-Johnson

BrightPoint Press

San Diego, CA

© 2024 BrightPoint Press
an imprint of ReferencePoint Press, Inc.
Printed in the United States

For more information, contact:
BrightPoint Press
PO Box 27779
San Diego, CA 92198
www.BrightPointPress.com

LIBRARY OF CONGRESS CATALOGING-IN-PUBLICATION DATA

Names: Crooks-Johnson, Jenny, author.
Title: Life in the Marine Force Recon / by Jenny Crooks-Johnson.
Description: San Diego, CA: BrightPoint Press, 2024. | Series: Life in the special forces |
    Includes bibliographical references and index. | Audience: Grades 7–9
Identifiers: LCCN 2023036215 (print) | LCCN 2023036216 (eBook) | ISBN 9781678207502
    (hardcover) | ISBN 9781678207519 (eBook)
Subjects: LCSH: United States. Marine Corps. Force Reconnaissance--Juvenile literature.
    | United States. Marine Corps--Commando troops--Juvenile literature. | Special forces
    (Military science)--United States--Juvenile literature.
Classification: LCC VE23 .C775 2024 (print) | LCC VE23 (eBook) | DDC 359.9/60973--dc23/
    eng/20230817
LC record available at https://lccn.loc.gov/2023036215
LC eBook record available at https://lccn.loc.gov/2023036216

CONTENTS

AT A GLANCE

- The Marine Force Recon is one of the US military's special forces.

- It operates under the command of the Marines. Recon Marines mainly support Marine missions.

- Marine Force Recon missions often take team members far behind enemy lines to perform reconnaissance, or recon.

- The Marine Force Recon also performs raids and other combat missions.

- All Recon Marines must pass the Basic Reconnaissance Course. It includes some of the most difficult training the US military offers.

- Recon Marines use equipment and vehicles designed to help them perform their jobs.

- There are three active Marine Force Recon battalions. Two are based in the United States, and one is based in Japan.

- Marine Force Recon battalions are divided into companies. Companies are divided into platoons, which are divided into teams.

- Teams perform the reconnaissance missions. Platoons support teams with special skills such as communications or logistics.

INTRODUCTION

SWIFT, SILENT, AND DEADLY

Sergeant Will Johnson parachutes 1,500 feet (457 meters) from a military helicopter. He lands in the cold ocean. His six-man Marine Force Recon team begins the 1.24-mile (2-km) swim to shore. The team members move at night to stay hidden. They wear special dive gear that leaves no trace of air bubbles. They push **rucksacks** in front of them. These bags are full of supplies, such as cameras and radios.

The team members rise onto the shore. They hold M4 carbine rifles. They hope the enemy will never know they were there. But they must be prepared. The Marine Force Recon's motto is "Swift, Silent, and Deadly."

Recon Marines must complete extensive training before they are allowed to parachute on missions.

The special force soldiers move toward the foreign enemy camp. Their mission is to gather information about the leader. They also need to report on the **terrain** and rivers they cross. Information about enemy forces and territory is called reconnaissance, or recon. Commanders will use the recon the team gathers to plan a raid. They hope to surprise the enemy and capture the leader.

The team finds the perfect place to watch the camp. They then dig hiding spots. Night-vision binoculars help them watch the enemy in darkness. The soldiers take photos. They also write reports in their hiding spots about what they see.

After two days, the team has enough recon. They know where the leader sleeps. They know the weapons he

Night-vision technology works by sensing small amounts of light that reflect off objects. The equipment then amplifies that light into a glowing green image.

carries. They know his habits. They also know the terrain and rivers the Marine raid team must cross. Sergeant Johnson is the radio operator on the team. He uses a satellite radio to send their recon back to commanders.

Marine Force Recon teams often insert into missions by water. Combat rubber raiding craft can help them quietly reach shorelines.

WHAT IS MARINE FORCE RECON?

The Marine Force Recon is one of the US military's special forces. It is commanded by the Marines. The teams get the recon that Marine commanders need to plan missions. Sometimes they perform missions alongside special forces from the other military branches.

Collecting recon is challenging work. Marine Force Recon teams must often sneak far behind enemy lines. They also perform some missions where combat is likely.

Recon Marines need great physical and mental strength. They also need in-depth training and special equipment. The most important skill Recon Marines need is the ability to work well together as a team.

1
MARINE FORCE RECON TRAINING

Marine Force Recon training is among the hardest training the US military offers. People who want to join must be prepared to overcome physical and mental challenges. The main training course to become a Recon Marine is the Basic Reconnaissance Course (BRC). It takes place in Pendleton, California.

However, there is a lot of testing and training before BRC.

BEFORE BRC

Everyone who wants to join the Marines must first take the Armed Services Vocational Aptitude Battery test (ASVAB).

The Basic Reconnaissance Course is held at Camp Pendleton on the southern coast of California.

All marines must pass the Physical Fitness Test. But Recon Marines pride themselves on surpassing the test's requirements.

A high ASVAB score gives marines more opportunities. Recon Marines must get the highest ASVAB scores of all.

The ASVAB has many parts. Recon Marines must score especially high on the General/Technical (GT) section. It measures reading, language, and math skills. These are skills Recon Marines need on missions.

Recon Marines must earn a GT score of at least 110.

People who want to join the Marines must also take the physical fitness test (PFT). It includes push-ups, **planks**, and a timed 3-mile (5-km) run. It also includes heavy lifting. A perfect PFT score is 300. Recon Marines must score at least 225. But most marines who succeed at BRC have scores of 285 or higher.

Recruiters are marines who encourage people to join the Marine Corps. They look for recruits who are well suited for Recon. The recruiters give contracts to interested recruits who score the highest.

Recruits with Recon contracts get to attend BRC. But they must first pass boot camp and the School of Infantry (SOI). During boot camp, marines run, swim, and do push-ups. They also do other physical exercises to get stronger. They learn basic combat and **marksmanship** skills.

During SOI, students do more physical exercise and combat training. They also retake the physical and mental enlistment tests. In addition, they take swimming and marksmanship tests. Marines who didn't get a Recon contract during recruitment can apply for Recon again during SOI. But they must have high enough GT and PFT scores. They must also pass an interview with Recon commanders. Marines who don't qualify for Recon training get other Marine assignments. But they can still try to join Recon later.

Recon training begins with BRC. The first part of BRC is the Reconnaissance Training Assessment Program (RTAP). It is meant

Many Marine Force Recon missions involve no fighting. But Recon Marines must learn marksmanship for when combat is necessary.

to push students to their limits. BRC staff sergeant Travis K. Nardi says, "Choosing Recon may be the first step in one of the best, most fulfilling life decisions you ever make. . . . You need to [know] it will take all you have to graduate."[1]

Recon Marines perform amphibious missions. This means the missions happen

It takes a lot of training to learn to swim while wearing a full uniform. The clothing creates resistance, making it harder to glide through the water.

on both land and water. Often, Recon Marines swim in rough seas carrying heavy rucksacks. RTAP begins by testing strength and swimming skills. Only students who pass these tests move on.

RTAP students exercise up to six hours per day. Some of this training takes place in a pool. For example, students dive to the bottom to get rubber rifles and heavy bricks. This training takes place in 16.5 feet (5 m) of water. Students also tread water while holding up the bricks and rubber rifles. They do these pool exercises in full uniforms, including boots.

Recon Marines also need land skills. RTAP teaches marines land and mountain navigation. It also teaches students how to tie a variety of knots. In fact, Recon Marines are often called ropers. This is because they have a rope tied around their bodies as they walk around the base. It is used to practice knots. Recon Marines must tie knots quickly.

Students also learn how to patrol. Students perform long hikes with heavy rucksacks. One RTAP student said, "All of the instructors keep pushing you to the point where you feel like quitting, but you know you won't. If you want to be a Recon Marine that's what it takes."[2] Many people do quit. More than half of students drop out or fail RTAP. Those who pass move on to BRC.

BASIC RECONNAISSANCE COURSE

The twelve-week BRC is the heart of Marine Force Recon training. It has three phases. The first phase focuses on individual skills. It starts with the Reconnaissance Physical Assessment Test (RPAT).

Students must swim 547 yards (500 m) in less than eleven minutes. They do timed push-ups, pull-ups, and sit-ups. They must then run 1.5 miles (2.4 km) in their uniforms. They must do this in less than eleven

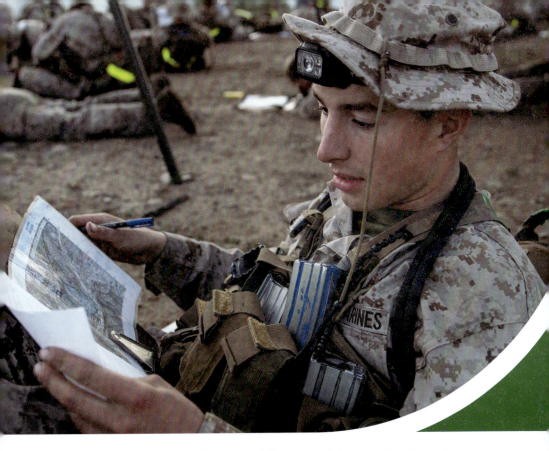

Land navigation is one of the most important parts of a Recon Marine's BRC training.

minutes. Next, they hike 12.4 miles (20 km) wearing a 50-pound (22.7-kg) rucksack. They do this in less than three hours. Finally, they move through two obstacle courses.

Students who fail get a second chance to pass the RPAT at the end of phase one. But failing again means losing the chance to become a Recon Marine. Even those who pass the RPAT must pass it again every year.

Recon Marines are trained to move in and out of enemy territory quickly. These movements are called insertions and extractions. During phase one, students learn an insertion method called fast roping. They slide down a rope that dangles from a helicopter. They also learn shooting and

ADDITIONAL RECON TRAINING

Recon Marines get even more training after BRC. They learn dive insertions at Combatant Dive School. They learn parachute insertions at Army Airborne Jump School. They learn to escape capture at Survival, Evade, Resistance and Escape School. After that, they can choose from many other courses.

explosives skills. In addition, they practice kicking in the ocean for long distances with fins. They do all these things while wearing uniforms and heavy rucksacks.

Phase two is the team phase. Students learn to work as a team. They also learn to silently communicate on patrols. They do timed hikes. And they learn more about using recon equipment. For example, they learn to use cameras and lenses to take photos. They also learn to hide well.

The final phase of BRC is the amphibious phase. Students gain ocean skills. They learn to drive rafts and boats. They learn to perform visit, board, search, and seizure (VBSS) raids. VBSS raids may involve freeing ships from pirates. Recon Marines speed alongside the ships. Then they attach ladders for climbing onto the watercraft.

Pirates are an ongoing threat on the world's oceans. VBSS training teaches Recon Marines how to take ships back from these criminals.

Recon Marine students must learn how to move through the ocean **surf zone**. They use fins to swim long distances with their rucksacks. In addition, they learn about beach terrain for performing recon work. This information tells commanders whether Marine vehicles can safely use certain beaches.

At the end of BRC, there is a big celebration. Students take off their ropes. The marines are not called ropers anymore. They know their knots and so much more. They now belong to the Marine Force Recon community. They are assigned to one of the US Marines' three Recon **battalions**.

2

EQUIPMENT AND VEHICLES

Recon Marines need certain types of equipment and vehicles for each mission. Most of their assignments are green side military operations. Green side means they hope never to shoot a bullet. In fact, they hope the enemy never knows they were there. During other operations, Recon Marines expect combat situations. VBSS operations are one example.

Recon Marines call these black side, or direct-action, missions.

Recon Marines must also adapt to changing war technology. Using the latest equipment and vehicles helps them

Although many of their missions are peaceful, Recon Marines are considered among the deadliest fighters in the US Marine Corps.

succeed. Marine general David H. Berger says, "War in the future will be much different than that of the recent past."[3] He explains that technology is advancing fast. It will have a big effect on war itself.

RECON EQUIPMENT

Recon Marines usually carry two guns. The M18 pistol works well for close combat. Recon Marines can attach lights or lasers to help them aim. Another common weapon is the M4A1 carbine. A carbine is a gun that has a shorter barrel than other rifles. The M4A1 carbine is lightweight and has many helpful attachments.

Among them are suppressor attachments, which reduce the light and sound from gunfire. Suppressors help

Special forces members can carry only so much equipment with them into the field. Having a grenade launcher attachment for their rifles makes one weapon work for two purposes.

Recon Marines fire their weapons without giving away their location. The M4A1 carbine also has an attachment that launches grenades. The grenade launcher has a laser sight for better aim.

The M4A1 carbine also has helpful gun sight attachments, which help shooters aim. These sights use lasers and night vision. These features help Recon Marines hit their targets, even in dark or smoky conditions. The scope has an adjustable zoom. Marines can change the setting based on the distance to the target. This helps them strike both nearby and distant targets.

MINI DRONES FOR RECON

Some Recon Marines use mini drones to get recon. These small devices can reach places that would be too risky for the marines to go. For instance, a mini drone can fly over a building or hill to see a target or threat.

Many missions take place at night. Night-vision goggles help Recon Marines see in very dark conditions. These goggles create images by combining heat sensors and tiny amounts of light. They can even work with only starlight. Thermal sensors show the heat that people and objects give off. This helps Recon Marines find hidden explosives or even distant enemies. Nia Cherry is a marine who works on weapons. She says the goggles "[intensify] Marines' ability to see anything in dark conditions, rain, fog, dust, smoke and through bushes."[4]

Recon Marines have equipment to help them hide and observe. They camouflage by attaching grass and plants to their clothing. These outfits are called ghillie suits. Recon Marines also use thermal telescopes to watch the enemy. Thermal cameras let them take pictures at night. Another important piece of equipment is a tough laptop. This computer helps Recon Marines write reports anywhere. When the reports are finished, the marines read them to commanders over radios.

Recon Marines also have special gear for insertions and extractions. For example, their dive gear includes a rebreather. This device removes carbon dioxide from marines' own recycled air. This allows them to keep breathing the same air. No air bubbles escape to give away their location. With a rebreather, Recon Marines can stay underwater for hours.

Sometimes, Recon Marines insert from airplanes as high as 30,000 feet (9,140 m). These insertions are called high-altitude, low-opening (HALO) airplane jumps.

Ghillie suits make it possible for special forces members to blend into their surroundings in the field.

Usually, they are done at night to avoid being seen. Recon Marines wait to open their parachutes until they are close to the ground. This also helps them avoid being seen. HALO jumps require Recon Marines to use oxygen. They also use helmets and flight suits that resist the freezing temperatures. Recon Marines have **GPS** devices to navigate in air, over land, and on water.

RECON VEHICLES

Many Marine Force Recon missions are amphibious. Recon Marines use both sea and land vehicles for this reason. The combat rubber raider craft is a popular choice for many operations. It is lightweight and fast. It can launch onto the ocean

MARINE FORCE RECON INSIGNIA

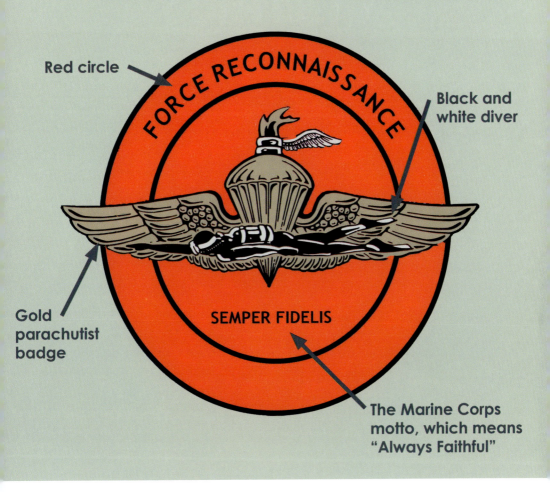

Red circle

Black and white diver

Gold parachutist badge

FORCE RECONNAISSANCE

SEMPER FIDELIS

The Marine Corps motto, which means "Always Faithful"

The Marine Force Recon insignia is a symbol of this special forces group.

from a Navy ship. It can also launch

from a submarine and be inflated on the

water's surface. Recon Marines can also

LAVs can often be transported to mission locations on military airplanes.

deflate the raft and sink it underwater. This helps them hide it while they perform recon. They then reinflate it when they return.

On land, Recon Marines often drive a light armored vehicle (LAV). This vehicle can be driven on challenging terrain. It also moves easily through all types of weather. It can even get across rivers. It has night vision and a powerful chain gun. However, Recon Marines mostly use the LAV to move quickly.

In 2023, the US Marine Corps was testing an advanced reconnaissance vehicle (ARV). But the ARV may be too heavy for missions in the Pacific. *Defense News* journalist Megan Eckstein writes, "Other solutions could include light and ultra-light tactical vehicles and small boats."[5]

3

MARINE FORCE RECON ROLES

Recon Marines must trust one another with their lives. Teams spend years training together. On deep recon missions, Recon Marines may have only each other. They may be far away from naval ships or air support.

Recon Marines know that other special forces depend on their work. These marines will not give up until they get the recon they need. They have a **creed** that states they will "adapt and do whatever it takes to complete the mission."[6]

There are three Marine Force Recon battalions. One is based in Camp Pendleton, California. The second is at Camp Lejeune in Jacksonville,

When a new officer takes over a Marine Force Recon battalion, a change-of-command ceremony marks the occasion.

North Carolina. And the third is located at Camp Schwab in Okinawa, Japan.

Recon Marines are dispatched to support Marine expeditionary forces (MEF). An MEF includes Navy ships, aircraft, and land vehicles. It has a commanding general. It also includes thousands of marines and sailors. Marines in an MEF are divided into companies. Recon Marines make up one of these companies.

FORCE RECON COMPANY ROLES

A Recon company has a commanding officer and a sergeant major. It also includes support marines with extra training. For example, these marines may specialize in communications or logistics. Each company also has five to six Recon platoons.

Major Jeffrey Erb became the commanding officer for the 1st Reconnaissance Battalion in Pendleton, California, in 2019.

Each Recon platoon has a commanding officer and a sergeant. It also has Recon Marines with supporting roles. One Recon Marine has extra training with radios. A different one specializes in keeping other equipment ready and repaired.

Enemies are less likely to spot small Marine Force Recon teams.

They support the three Recon teams that are also part of the platoon.

FORCE RECON TEAM ROLES

Marine Force Recon teams are the eyes and ears of their commanders. Most teams have four to six marines. However, some missions require up to twelve Marines per team. Staff Sergeant Jonathan E. Wood thinks small recon teams have an advantage. He says that they are "able to get very close to the enemy without being detected."[7] A small team is less likely to be seen by the enemy.

One team member is the point person. This marine finds the best path forward. The point person is always on the lookout for enemy forces. Explosives and other dangers are a constant threat. The point person's training in tactics and leadership helps keep the team safe.

The team leader keeps the point person in sight. The other team members follow the leader. This keeps the team together and on task as they patrol.

The radio operator sends recon to commanders over the radios. This marine may also call for help if the team comes under attack. The radio operator carries radios, antennae, and batteries. There is often an assistant radio operator, as well.

All team members carry rucksacks full of equipment. These bags can weigh 90 to 120 pounds (40–55 kg). However, one team member carries extra equipment. This is called the slack person. This Recon Marine may carry heavier weapons, such as a machine gun. He or she also carries extra ammunition and batteries.

The assistant team leader follows behind the rest of the team. Like the others, this marine carefully patrols. Part of the assistant team leader's job is making sure no one

Using explosives to blast through doorways is called breaching.

is left behind. This person also supervises other team members.

Recon teams sometimes need members with extra training. For instance, a ship-boarding mission might need a point person who is also a sniper. The mission might need a team leader who is trained in explosives to get through doors and windows.

A deep recon mission might need a slack person who is also trained to operate

ALEXA BARTH: FIRST FEMALE RECON MARINE

Until 2019, all Recon Marines were men. Alexa Barth changed this when she became the first woman to complete the BRC. Barth joined the 1st Recon Battalion in California.

drones. It might need a radio operator with skills in tactical air control. This person communicates with aircraft overhead and helps planes land. A team might even need a Recon Marine trained in foreign weapons.

Most Marine Force Recon missions are considered a success when no shots are fired. Marine Eric O'Neil stresses that this special force's purpose is gathering recon. He says, "Marines in Force Recon are absolutely trained in direct action missions, and are capable of performing in combat situations, but that is not their primary role."[8]

Force Recon companies, platoons, and teams adapt as needed. They never give up. Their work makes it possible for other Marines to do their jobs.

4

MARINE FORCE RECON IN ACTION

The Marine Force Recon has been in service since 1943. During World War II, these marines did recon to find enemy locations. They identified which beaches were safest for Marine vehicles to use. They also gathered recon about the best aircraft landing sites.

Since then, Recon Marines have done many more missions. The public hears more about Force Recon black side missions than its green side missions. Green side missions involve methods Recon Marines want to keep secret. They don't want enemies to find out how they gather recon.

Black side missions make the news more often than green side missions. But Recon Marines aren't upset by this because they want their recon work to remain secret.

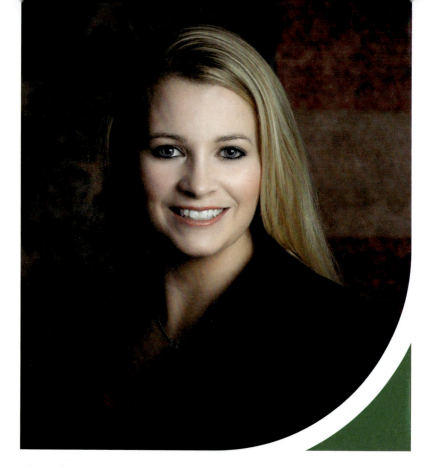

After her 2003 rescue, Jessica Lynch went on to become a fifth-grade teacher.

RESCUING PRIVATE JESSICA LYNCH

In 2003, the United States and Iraq were at war. Recon Marines joined other special forces on a black side mission. Nineteen-year-old Private Jessica Lynch was serving in the US Army in Iraq. In March, her military vehicle was **ambushed**.

She was injured and taken captive. The Iraqis held Private Lynch in a hospital in An-Nasiriyah.

The Marines learned where Private Lynch was. They planned a night raid on the hospital. The goal was to rescue Private Lynch and any other US soldiers held there. First, the 15th MEU Marines attacked a bridge near the hospital. Shortly after, artillery and aircraft attacked other enemy buildings. Both attacks were to distract Iraqi troops.

Army Rangers landed west of the hospital. They provided security. They also prepared an emergency landing site for the rescue helicopter. The 2nd Force Recon Company performed recon on the rescue site. This information helped commanders plan the raid.

Snipers in the Marine Force Recon are always prepared to use their skills for hostage rescue.

Marine Force Recon snipers were ready to shoot if needed. Other Recon Marines guided the emergency helicopters into the landing site. Some Recon Marines drove a vehicle with a machine gun to attack the hospital. MEU tanks also attacked the hospital.

US Navy SEALs entered the hospital. They fought their way to Private Lynch. She said, "It had all felt unreal, these men standing beside me and telling me they were Americans."[9] Within 25 minutes, she was flying in a helicopter on her way to a hospital in Germany.

Everyone celebrated the rescue. But they were not done. Recon Marines helped the 15th MEU rebuild An-Nasiriyah. They wanted to form a better relationship with the Iraqi people.

THE *MAGELLAN STAR*

In September 2010, Recon Marines performed another black side mission. Somali pirates took over a German cargo ship named the *Magellan Star* in the

As ships and planes distracted the pirates aboard the Magellan Star, Recon Marines came alongside the vessel. They used their VBSS skills to take control of it.

Indian Ocean. It was 85 miles (136 km) southeast of Yemen. The ship's crew locked themselves in a room and called for help.

The 15th MEU was on the job. It had a platoon of 24 Force Recon Marines aboard a nearby Navy ship, the USS *Dubuque*. The Recon platoon sergeant ordered the teams to get ready. They double-checked their equipment. Then they got the final order. Early the next morning, they set out to rescue the *Magellan Star*.

MEU airplanes and the USS *Dubuque* distracted the pirates. The Recon Marines sped to the *Magellan Star* on their combat rubber raiding crafts. Snipers covered them. The Recon Marines threw ladders over the side of the boat. Then they climbed aboard. They had their rifles ready. Some pirates quickly surrendered. The Recon Marines chased others down. The mission was a success. The Recon Marines captured all the pirates without firing a shot.

Serving in the Marine Force Recon isn't easy. It takes all a marine can give. But Recon Marines are ready for the challenge. Overcoming challenges is a part of who they are. They serve anywhere they are

FORCE RECON MAJOR JAMES CAPERS JR.

Major James Capers Jr. was born to a family of poor sharecroppers. He served in the 3rd Force Recon Company during the Vietnam War (1954–1975). Capers performed many difficult missions. In 1966, he became the first Black American to command a Recon company. Capers received many awards for his service, including three Purple Hearts, two Bronze Stars, and a Silver Star.

Marine Force Recon teams spend a great deal of time training, so they are ready to serve when they are needed. Sometimes, they use role playing for learning purposes.

needed for as long as it takes to finish

each mission.

GLOSSARY

ambushed
surprised by an attack

battalions
large groups of troops ready for battle

creed
a statement of beliefs and values

GPS (global positioning system)
a network of satellites that send signals to devices on the ground to determine the devices' locations

marksmanship
skill in shooting

planks
exercises consisting of holding a position similar to a push-up for as long as possible

rucksacks
backpacks designed to carry heavy loads

surf zone
a place where ocean waves get taller and break

terrain
physical features of a stretch of land

SOURCE NOTES

CHAPTER ONE: MARINE FORCE RECON TRAINING

1. Travis K. Nardi, *All It Takes: Become a Recon Marine*. Scotts Valley, CA: CreateSpace Independent Publishing, 2021, p. 3.

2. Quoted in Luke Kuennen, "Marines Prepare for Basic Reconnaissance Course," *US Department of Defense*, January 31, 2018. www.defense.gov.

CHAPTER TWO: EQUIPMENT AND VEHICLES

3. David H. Berger, "Together We Must Design the Future Force," *US Naval Institute*, November 2019. www.usni.org.

4. Quoted in Kaitlin Kelly, "Next Gen Binoculars Increase Survivability for Recon, EODM Marines," *US Marine Corps*, June 19, 2018. www.marines.mil.

5. Megan Eckstein, "Marine Corps Pushes 'Dramatic Change' for Its Reconnaissance Forces," *Defense News*, June 5, 2023. www.defensenews.com.

CHAPTER THREE: MARINE FORCE RECON ROLES

6. "Reconnaissance Creed," *US Marines*, n.d. www.marines.mil.

7. Quoted in Pete Nealen, "What a USMC Recon Team Looks Like," *SOFREP*, April 4, 2013. www.sofrep.com.

8. Eric O'Neil, "Where Does Marine Force Recon Fit in the World of Special Operations?" *Forbes*, March 1, 2012. www.forbes.com.

CHAPTER FOUR: MARINE FORCE RECON IN ACTION

9. Quoted in Hollie McKay, "Former POW Jessica Lynch on Surviving Captivity, Getting Through the Dark Days, and Fulfilling Her Lifelong Dream," *Coffee or Die*, April 29, 2021. www.coffeeordie.com.

FOR FURTHER RESEARCH

BOOKS

Tammy Gagne, *Life as a Navy SEAL*. San Diego, CA: BrightPoint Press, 2024.

Percy Leed, *The US Marine Corps in Action*. Minneapolis, MN: Lerner, 2023.

Howard Phillips, *Inside Marine Force Recon*. New York: PowerKids Press, 2022.

INTERNET SOURCES

"Basic Reconnaissance Course Preparation," *United States Marines*, n.d. www.tecom.marines.mil.

David H. Berger, "Together We Must Design the Future Force," *US Naval Institute*, November 2019. www.usni.org.

"Force Recon Overview," *Military.com*, n.d. www.military.com.

WEBSITES

Marines.com
www.marines.com

This is the official US Marine Corps recruiting website. It has information about joining the Marines.

Military.com
www.military.com

This is a news and resource website about the military. It contains information about the history, training, and organization of the Marine Force Recon.

United States Marines
www.marines.mil

This is the official website of the US Marines. It includes news and articles about the Marine Force Recon.

INDEX

IMAGE CREDITS

ABOUT THE AUTHOR

Jenny Crooks-Johnson is an elementary education teacher who writes fiction and nonfiction books for children. She lives in Colorado with her amazing family. She would like to thank Recon gunnery sergeant Travis K. Nardi for his help with this book. She would also like to thank her writing group, the PBJs, for their support. She would especially like to thank all US military members, including those in her own family, for their dedicated service.